Editor
Eric Migliaccio

Managing Editor
Ina Massler Levin, M.A.

Editor-in-Chief
Sharon Coan, M.S. Ed.

Illustrator
Bruce Hedges

Cover Artist
Janet Chadwick

Art Coordinator
Kevin Barnes

Art Director
CJae Froshay

Imaging
Ralph Olmedo, Jr.
Rosa C. See

Product Manager
Phil Garcia

Publishers
Mary D. Smith, M.S. Ed.

Author

Teacher Created Resources Staff

Teacher Created Resources, Inc.
6421 Industry Way
Westminster, CA 92683
www.teachercreated.com
©2003 Teacher Created Resources, Inc.
Reprinted, 2004
Made in the U.S.A.
ISBN-0-7439-3769-4

Table of Contents

Introduction

The old adage "practice makes perfect" can really hold true for your child and his or her education. The more practice and exposure your child has with concepts being taught in school, the more success he or she is likely to find. For many parents, knowing how to help their children may be frustrating because the resources may not be readily available.

As a parent, it is also difficult to know where to focus your efforts so that the extra practice your child receives at home supports what he or she is learning in school.

This book has been written to help parents and teachers reinforce basic skills with children. *Practice Makes Perfect: Modern Cursive* helps children learn to correctly form the uppercase and lowercase forms of each letter. The exercises in this book can be done sequentially or can be taken out of order, as needed.

The following standards or objectives will be met or reinforced by completing the practice pages included in this book. These standards and objectives are similar to the ones required by your state and school district.

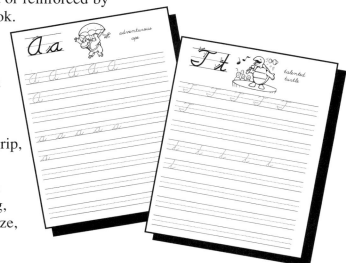

- The student will demonstrate competence in writing the cursive forms of each uppercase and lowercase letter.

- The student will increase control of pencil grip, paper position, stroke, and posture.

- The student will demonstrate competence in writing words legibly in cursive handwriting, using correct letter formation, appropriate size, and spacing.

How to Make the Most of This Book

Here are some useful ideas for making the most of this book:

- Set aside a specific place in your home to work on this book. Keep it neat and tidy, with the necessary materials on hand.

- Set up a certain time of day to work on these practice pages to establish consistency, or look for times in your day or week that are less hectic and more conducive to practicing skills.

- Keep all practice sessions with your child positive and constructive. If your child becomes frustrated or tense, set the book aside and look for another time to practice. Forcing your child to perform will not help. Do not use this book as a punishment.

- Help beginning readers with instructions.

- Review the work your child has done.

- Pay attention to the areas in which your child has the most difficulty. Provide extra guidance and exercises in those areas.

- Look for ways to make real-life application to the skills being reinforced. Play games such as having your child write lists with you.

The Alphabet

Aa   Bb   Cc   Dd

Ee   Ff   Gg   Hh

Ii   Jj   Kk   Ll

Mm   Nn   Oo   Pp

Qq   Rr   Ss   Tt

Uu   Vv   Ww   Xx

Yy   Zz

Lines and Loops

Curves

C C C

c c c

c c c

nnnn

n n n

mmmm

adventurous
ape

a a a a a

a

a a a a a

a

B b

bashful
bat

B   B   B   B   B

B

b   b   b   b   b

b

cautious
camel

C C C C C

C

c c c c c

c

  *dynamic duck*

$\mathcal{D}$ $\mathcal{D}$ $\mathcal{D}$ $\mathcal{D}$ $\mathcal{D}$

$\mathcal{D}$

d d d d d

d

energetic
elf

E E E E E

E

e e e e e

e

2

3 1

*floating
feather*

𝓕 𝓕 𝓕 𝓕 𝓕

𝓕

𝒻 𝒻 𝒻 𝒻 𝒻

𝒻

gleeful
goat

$\mathcal{G}$ $\mathcal{G}$ $\mathcal{G}$ $\mathcal{G}$ $\mathcal{G}$

$\mathcal{G}$

g g g g g

g

haunted
helicopter

H   H   H   H   H

H

h   h   h   h   h

h

inventive
insect

ℓ ℓ ℓ ℓ ℓ

ℓ

i i i i i

i

J j

jolly
jellyfish

kindhearted
kitten

K K K K K

K

k k k k k

k

lazy
leprechaun

$\mathcal{L}$ $\mathcal{L}$ $\mathcal{L}$ $\mathcal{L}$ $\mathcal{L}$ $\mathcal{L}$

$\mathcal{L}$

ℓ ℓ ℓ ℓ ℓ ℓ

ℓ

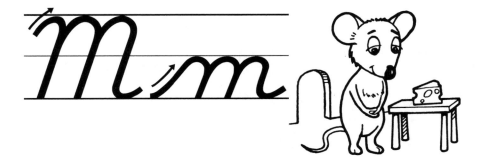

modest
mouse

$\mathcal{M}$ $\mathcal{M}$ $\mathcal{M}$ $\mathcal{M}$ $\mathcal{M}$

$\mathcal{M}$

m m m m m

m

$\mathcal{N}$ n

noisy
nest

n n n n n

n

n n n n n

n

old
ostrich

$\mathcal{O}$ $\mathcal{O}$ $\mathcal{O}$ $\mathcal{O}$ $\mathcal{O}$

$\mathcal{O}$

$\mathcal{O}$ $\mathcal{O}$ $\mathcal{O}$ $\mathcal{O}$ $\mathcal{O}$

$\mathcal{O}$

perfect pumpkin

P   P   P   P   P

P

p   p   p   p   p

p

quiet
queen

2   2   2   2   2

2

q   q   q   q   q

q

rich

raccoon

R R R R R

R

r r r r r

r

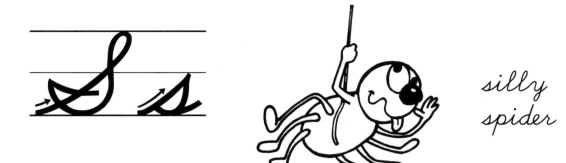

silly
spider

$\mathscr{S}$ $\mathscr{S}$ $\mathscr{S}$ $\mathscr{S}$ $\mathscr{S}$

$\mathscr{S}$

s s s s s

s

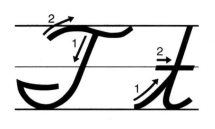 

talented
turtle

$\mathcal{T}$ $\mathcal{T}$ $\mathcal{T}$ $\mathcal{T}$ $\mathcal{T}$ $\mathcal{T}$

$\mathcal{T}$

t t t t t

t

uncertain
umpire

𝒰 𝒰 𝒰 𝒰 𝒰

𝒰

𝓊 𝓊 𝓊 𝓊 𝓊

𝓊

valuable

vehicle

𝒱 𝒱 𝒱 𝒱 𝒱

𝒱

𝓋 𝓋 𝓋 𝓋 𝓋

𝓋

wacky
walrus

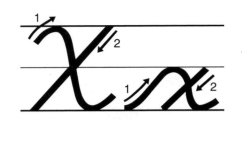

extraordinary
xylophone

$\mathcal{X}$ $\mathcal{X}$ $\mathcal{X}$ $\mathcal{X}$ $\mathcal{X}$

$\mathcal{X}$

x x x x x

x

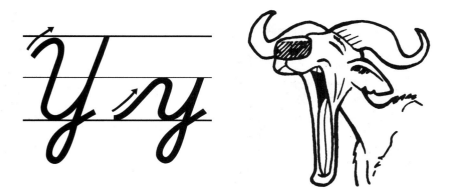

Yy

yawning
yak

Y Y Y Y Y

Y

y y y y y

y

Zz Zz

zany
zebra

Z Z Z Z Z

Z

Z Z Z Z Z

Z

Ascenders

b

d

f

h

k

l

t

Descenders

g

j

p

q

y

z

g   j   p   q   y   z

Consonant Combinations

bl   bl

block

fl   fl

flower

gl   gl

globe

Consonant Combinations *(cont.)*

br   br

bread

cr   cr

crown

dr   dr

drum

Consonant Combinations *(cont.)*

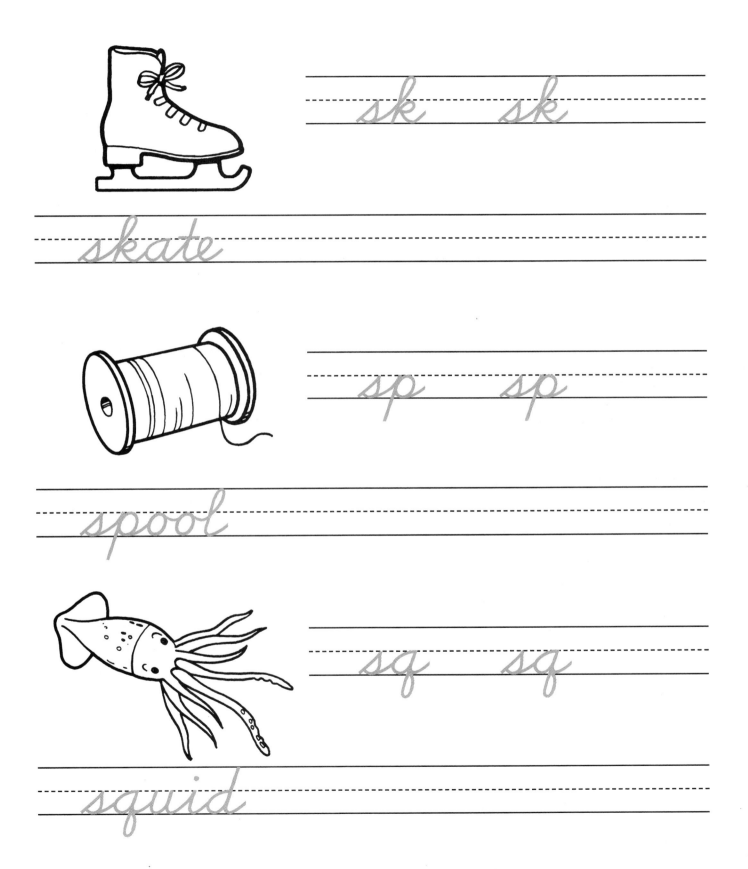

sk   sk

skate

sp   sp

spool

sq   sq

squid

Consonant Combinations *(cont.)*

ch   ch

chair

sh   sh

shell

wh   wh

whale

Consonant Combinations *(cont.)*

kn   kn

knight

mb   mb

lamb

wr   wr

wrist

Consonant Combinations *(cont.)*

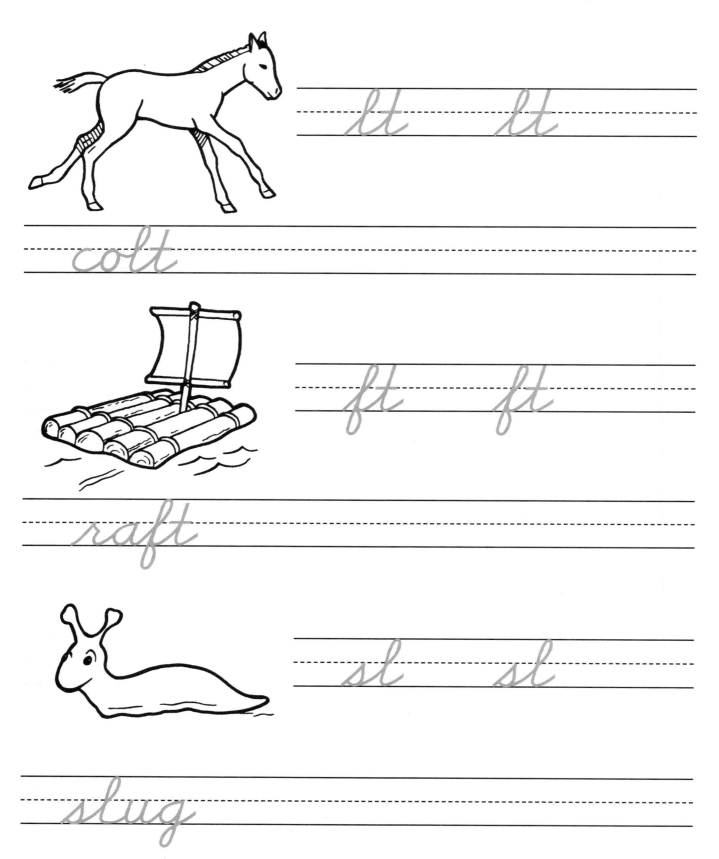

_tt_   _tt_

colt

_ft_   _ft_

raft

_sl_   _sl_

slug

Vowel Combinations

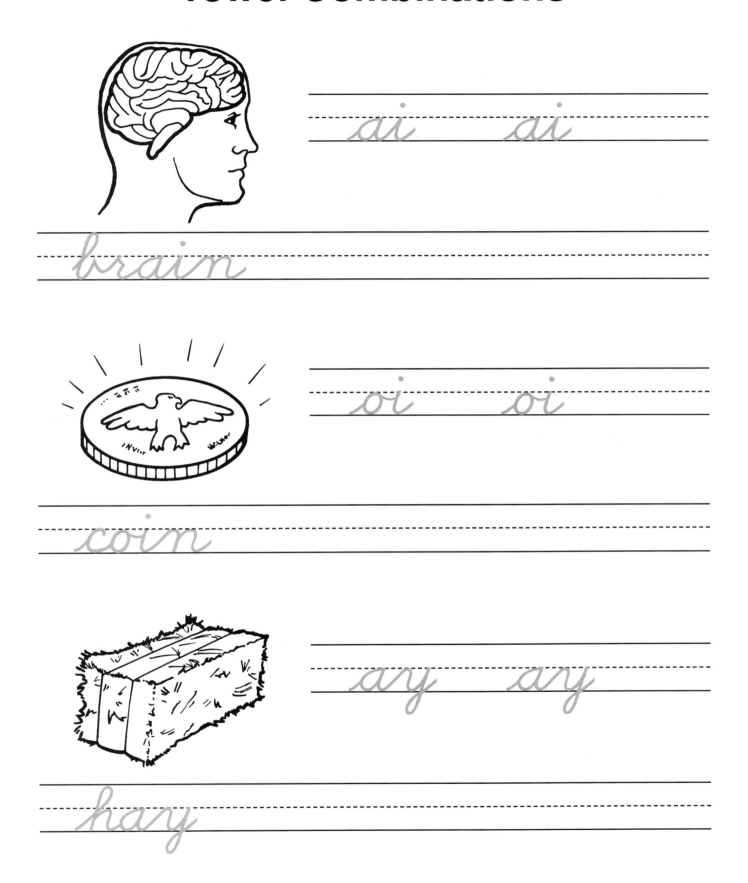

ai   *ai*

brain

oi   *oi*

coin

ay   *ay*

hay

Vowel Combinations *(cont.)*

read

ea   ea

teach

ee   ee

deer

ie   ie

shield

Vowel Combinations *(cont.)*

oa   oa

goat

oo   oo

tool

ou   ou

mouse

Days of the Week

Sunday

Monday

Tuesday

Wednesday

Thursday

Friday

Saturday

Months of the Year

January

February

March

April

May

June

Months of the Year *(cont.)*

July

August

September

October

November

December

Practice Page

January
Sunday
February
Monday
Tuesday
March
April
May
June
December
November
October
September
Wednesday
Thursday
Friday
Saturday
August
July

Today is a

_____

- - - - - - - - - - - - - -

_____

(day of the week)

in the month of

_____

- - - - - - - - - - - - - -

_____

(month of the year)

Practice Page *(cont.)*

Use this page to practice your handwriting.